phases

phases

tramaine suubi

AMISTAD

An Imprint of HarperCollins*Publishers*

PHASES. Copyright © 2025 by Tramaine Suubi. All rights reserved. Printed in the United States of America. No part of this book may be used or reproduced in any manner whatsoever without written permission except in the case of brief quotations embodied in critical articles and reviews. For information, address HarperCollins Publishers, 195 Broadway, New York, NY 10007.

HarperCollins books may be purchased for educational, business, or sales promotional use. For information, please email the Special Markets Department at SPsales@harpercollins.com.

FIRST EDITION

Designed by Yvonne Chan

Library of Congress Cataloging-in-Publication Data has been applied for.

ISBN 978-0-06-334491-4

24 25 26 27 28 LBC 5 4 3 2 1

to my Tash & my Titi, who loved me in every phase

The white fathers told us: I think, therefore I am.
The Black mother within each of us—the poet—whispers
in our dreams: I feel, therefore I can be free.

—Audre Lorde, "Poetry Is Not a Luxury"

phases

waning
gibbous

he & i

he frowns across from me
quiet, thinking
always thinking

i smile across from him
loud, feeling
always feeling

hands

here in this moment
screen on
lights off

you drifting off
me breathing still
head tucked in your heartbeat

memorizing your heartbeat
mind running in time
to your heartbeat
then—sleep

wrapped in feelings as we sleep
feelings so foreign that i actually
cannot sleep until i find your hands

holding

for the first time since knowing you
i am fast, asleep

for once, it is not a sunray
for once, it is not a bell
for once, it is not a bird

for the second time since missing you
i dream of you

for a second, it is just laughter
for a second, it is just mischief
for a second, it is just moonbeam

a deep sleep in arms besides my own
a deep sleep in a bed besides my own

& this is how it starts

two a.m.

you are telling me to act like nothing happened
you are telling me to grow up yet you play pretend
you are telling me so much in those empty words

my body disobeys, my mind resists
fights against purging you from my nervous system
constantly reminds me of how gently you held me
kept me spellbound with whispers of your lips
melted my skin into butter with the grip of your hands
derailed my thoughts with the gravel of your voice
explored the terrain of my body with divine patience
awakened parts of me after an eternity of hibernation
consumed me in a fog & left me gasping for air
drowning in the roar of my wildfire

i am asking you if something happened
i am asking you to be honest yet i live a lie
i am asking you too much in those heavy words

two p.m.

i patiently recollect that night
piece by piece
i find another fragment hidden away
in my thoughts every day
i remember how i shut my eyes when you
sighed & kissed me
i wish i had known you were being sealed in my memory

each time i disappeared in your arms
each time i was intoxicated
each i was infused with you
my name rolled off your tongue
slowly & carelessly
dripped raw honey on the blankets
the scent was clinging to everything

you set my midnights on fire
now the heat is invading my daydreams

my face was naked with want
now my skin is burning with need

you enter my thoughts & make yourself at home
you leave the door open & the chill of reality
trails in behind you
you spread out on my skin & become a warm quilt
a patchwork of things unsaid
you muffle the cold but you leave the door open
why do you leave the door open

sobering

i need to dance, with you fully sober
i want to hear our bodies heating
i want to hear our hearts beating
i just need to dance

i need to dance with you, fully sober
i do not want something twisting through your brain
i do not want something winding through my veins
i just need to dance with you

i need to dance with you fully, sober
i want to sink in your urgency
i want to sink in your sincerity
i just need to dance with you fully

i need to dance with you fully sober
i do not want to breathe in your lies
i do not want to breathe in your sighs
i just need to dance with you fully sober

addicting

i could not not choose you
despite the fact that i was drawn
to someone else
despite the fact that i nursed feelings
for someone else
i still chose you
i fought it at every turn
sobbed furiously
lashed out at God
foresaw nothing but devastation
for my wayward heart
felt my body groaning
preparing for undoing to come
yet i just could not not choose you

fantasies

i love you, i do not know for how long
nor do i understand why but i love you
you cross my mind every night
oftentimes in daydreams, too
they always start
& end with us
dancing

i always lost track of time
when i danced with you
i conjured up so many
duets for us in my
imagination, but
i must settle for
the ghosts of
what we were
dancing into
oblivion
never to
dance
to life
again

realities

i told you tonight
called you twice
mind breaking, body quaking
stated plainly, "i am in love with you"

"thank you for sharing that," you whispered
your voice as even as ever
"thank you for having the courage to share such difficult feelings"
really, that is all you had to say

as i drove home
i listened to one hymn over & over
as i walked home
i whispered one prayer over & over

God protect my heart
God protect my heart
cover me in your precious blood

fear of being unattractive
fear of being unwanted
fear of being unloved

these fears rang loud in my ears until i called you
you may not find me attractive
you may not want me
you may not even love me
but ever since that night these fears ring silent

my mind, mending, my body, believing
i think this, this is the beginning of freedom
from you

forget-me-nots

all the black boys i loved before
i loved myself
stroked & shattered my ego
these are the ones who could have been
the frederick bailey to my anna murray
i was groomed to be a kingmaker
but these three black boys were still boys
still reckless & careless
stayed stuck at their first heartbreak
whether it was
a white girl's lies or their father's pink slips
a white boy's ties or their mother's tight lips
they all shared the same predictable favorite
color: the blues

the boy from nola

i think of the boy from nola
the lost boy who lost
his father & his grandfather
in that order

i think of the boy from nola
who was chased by the hurricane
the one who was swept out west
who took his nostalgia
& channeled it into something
beautiful & bright, something orange

i think of the boy from nola
who cracked & let the endless water him
the one who swam good through the pain
transformed, came out
his hair blonded
his spirit lighted

i think of the boy from nola
who hollers & croons
when i cannot
who sighs & cries
when i cannot

i think of the boy from nola
the one who has had a hold
on me for three years running
the one who is shunning home
constantly humming in my mind

i think of the boy from nola
how one day, just one day
i would love to
hold his gaze
kiss him dazed
to sing thank you, thank you very much

love languages

maama is a daughter of the west
she speaks in long, flowing vowels
soft consonants
she speaks in a smooth waltz
invites you to join the dance

taata is a son of the east
he speaks in wide, staccato vowels
hard consonants
he speaks in a steady march
instructs you to fall in line

when she says, "ninkukunda munonga"
you translate, "i love you"
but i hear, "i like you so much"

when he says, "nkwagala nyo"
you translate, "i love you"
but i hear, "i want you so much"

half
moon

junction

caught between remembering to forget
& forgetting to remember

caught between drips of nostalgia
& drops of anticipation

caught between all that i am losing
& all that is finding me

caught between many spaces lately
but mostly caught between
thoughts of you & i

sweet nothings

they are not written in a love letter
they are not written in a cloud
they are not sung in a love song
they are not sung to me out loud

they are not shouted across the mountain
they are not shouted across the sea
they are not whispered under lamplight
they are not whispered under sheets

the sweetest nothings ever given to me

"para ti el mundo"

slip thoughtlessly through the hands of a boy
who is already giving the world to another girl

in another life

you see me & i feel seen
you hear me & i feel heard
you love me & i feel loved

i feel this peace
when i hear you speak
when i hear you laugh
i want to make you happy
i know i can make you happy
i have never known anything
in my life with such certainty

but from the moment i met you
you gave yourself so fully to her
i love you even more for that
i am keeping my distance only for that

i have never met a man like you
the whole of this life
i am terrified
i will never meet a man like you
for the rest of this life

the wisest man

i want to meet the wisest man who ever lived

i want to take a photograph of him & his father
the man after God's own heart
before everything fell apart

i want to take a photograph of him & his mother
a young widow & rape survivor
after she tells him what his father did to her

i want to ask him how it hurt to see
his carnal brother be the favorite son
of the Beloved king

i want to ask him how it hurt to kill
his mother's firstborn, the original heir
to his throne

i want to ask him if it was hard being
raised by the Beloved prophet
then being consumed by idols

i want to meditate with him in silence
wonder if he should have prayed
for something else besides wisdom

i want to know if he was ever in love
how his seven hundred wives
felt about love
if he asked them
if he cared

i want to know what sex meant to him
how his three hundred concubines
felt about sex
if he asked them
if he cared

i want to scream at him for using
among a thousand women
the queen of sheba
i want to wail at him for abandoning
his afrikan dynasty

i want to weep with him as he bitterly writes
proverb after proverb in the scriptures
hear the story behind every single one
i want to sit & listen to the man
who began with a song of songs
ended with ecclesiastes

i want to kneel at the table
of the wisest man who ever lived
lament how he spent his life
chasing after the wind

on the eighth day

the white man said, let us create money in our image
let us take its form & fold the lie until it fits
until it shrouds many to become one

& the white man said, let us create sex in our image
let us take its form & twist the connection until it fits
until we have exhausted every climax

& the white man said, let us create power in our image
let us take its form & shatter the illusion until it fits
until we are the very definition of supremacy

& the white man said, let us create God in our image
let us take their form & stretch their whole truth until it fits
until it is a manifestation of our destiny

taxi driver

"you are lost
>you are no longer afrikan

you are amerikkkan
>you are of the west

if you go back
>no one will accept you

you will have to
>prove yourself"

tropes

i want to cut the ropes in my mind
the ones that keep me down to earth
grounded in the reality of this body
i want to believe the fairy tales
the ones that demand my softness
keep my femininity pretty 'n' pink
i want to relish the happy ever afters
the ones that offer me a cruel high
extending the delusion of grandeur

yet

i am never the hero of the kingdom
i am always the dragon that must fall

i am never the princess with the golden hair
i am always the witch that must burn

i am never the blessing that saves
i am always the curse that kills

so

while you bemoan my suspension
of disbelief, with great exasperation
consider my skin, my hair, my eyes
& wonder why my belief is missing
in stories that do not believe in me

asphyxiation

to be afrikan in amerikkka
is to be born bronze, never to see the gold
yet still enter the race knowing how all shall unfold
is to absorb the blood, sweat & tears your mother
& father shed to plant you in this dying land
is to watch your golden ticket fade to rust
to become dust, on the "streets paved with gold"
is to realize, belatedly, that a poet told you
clearly warned you, "nothing gold can stay"
is to hear liberty declare, "bring me your tired
your poor, your huddled masses here"
is to learn that "here" you will be milked dry
drained of all the honey in your eyes
is to feel that you cannot bear even
the easy yoke & the light burden
is to watch the horror unfold
through cracked glasses of rose
is to live on copper, suffocated
by a leash of green
until you join the rat race
apparently the rats exist beyond
your canteen
your bungalow
your parliament
until you too become
a slave to the amerikkkan dream
the dream was not, is not & will not
ever be of you, by you, or for you people

until you feel the cold, hard reality
here will never fully embrace you
& there will never fully release you
to be afrikan in amerikkka
is to become stranded on a bridge
& to become a paradox
never quite enough, always too much
stuck between the damn golden door

homegone

i do not have a home
i have roots, i have family
i even have community
but i do not have a home

i do not have a home
i have a room, i have an apartment
i even have a permanent address
but i do not have a home

ten neighborhoods
three countries
two continents
all within the first twenty years
of my life on this earth
i fell in love with each one just
before i moved to the next one
i also fell in love with the lie
that home is where the heart is
but i cannot single out one
of the ten pieces of my heart
but i cannot stomach the ache
of ten heartbreaks

homesick

there is a kind of sickness that has no cure
affects your physical, mental, spiritual
health in ways you cannot imagine, cannot see
there is a kind of sickness that spills everywhere
colors your perspective for the rest of your life
there is a kind of sickness that can lie
dormant for years then crash over you
cling to your skin for days
there is a kind of sickness that seeps
the contentment from your spirit & wraps
you in a permanent air of restlessness
there is a kind of sickness that creates a chasm
brands you stranger no matter how familiar
there is a kind of sickness that comes in waves
& some nights you succumb to drowning

brink

i am an elastic winter
a shimmer of biting words
a glitter of disappointments
spread myself over the dead leaves
& sprawl myself over the dying trees
we sway, mourn in harmony
the leaves, the trees & my rubber knees
colors are too heavy to carry these days
so i wrap my legs & drape my arms
in the black
stretch myself over the brittle dust
& strain myself over the hard crust
we grind, heave a melody
the dust, the crust & my jagged trust
normalcy is too tight to wear these days
so i unknot my stomach & untie my spine

chicago

i was not supposed to fall in love with her

i became aware of her little quirks
how she danced easily from glee to elegance
i became accustomed to her gorgeous outline
how she lit up at night & became one with the stars
i became enamored with her dark waves
how they would glide in the long winters
i became desperate for her touch on my skin
how she felt on those golden mornings & silver afternoons

but i was not supposed to fall in love with her

waning
crescent

intuition

i am false, inauthentic
a lie in this white dress
i itch for the truth
know what lies beneath my all
a wanting, a deep longing
for the raw, the uncensored
i have primal instincts
& strange needs
my desires are sudden & acute
i want to meet them fully
live in the gray more than i want to
the more i grow, the less i know
i scratch at the truth
i am on the cusp of a great something
perpetually holding
my breath

after

we dance at the after party
we dwell on the after taste

we sleep during the after math
we stumble through the after shocks

we linger in the after hours
we listen to the after thoughts

daybreak

wake up high
feeling low
watch for moonset & begin
to resent the sunrise
my darkness gone too quick
the clouds catch fire & my resolve burns
with them
vaguely recall something
about green lights & blue eyes
sit in my holy lonely & breathe
long, coughing short
skin slick with sweat as i roll
over, taste the regret
in my cottoned mouth

daze

the dog days are here
& it is all too much
the air tastes heavy
my feet are molasses
& the midnight sirens
are particularly shrill
hear in technicolor
see in sharp textures
& dull angles
nothing feels real
my pain is a ticking clock
quiet, steady, always in the background
my train of thought runs in & out of focus
could be derailed at any minute really

here you are

here you are on a somber thursday mourning

your senses feel too sharp

your skin is too hot
your music is too loud
your streetlight is too bright
your drink is too bitter
your smoke is too sweet

you wonder who is dreaming about you
for a couple of hours
you wonder why God is punishing you
for a couple of minutes
you wonder what it feels like to feel nothing
for a couple of seconds

here you are again

here you are on a hazy friday evening
sipping pinot noir & listening to songs
you swore you would not play
turning off lights & making calls
you promised you would not make
tasting kisses you declared
you would not remember

you feel like warm tears
you feel like warm tears & anguish
you reek of plums
you reek of plums & pining
you sound like mysteries
you sound like unloved mysteries

here you are yet again

here you are on a lonely saturday mourning

you are stirring lukewarm soup
you are giving loose hugs & light kisses
you are giving halfheartedly
you swore you would never
give anyone half of a heart
you close your eyes as the golden leaves
are crumbling all around you

your body is cold, not numb
your mind is heavy, not blank
your heart is tired, not empty
your body will feel numb
when the blood runs cold
your mind will go blank
when the snow is heavy
your heart will drop empty
when the love grows tired

here you are one last time

here you are on a ragged sunday evening
you are folded on the floor of the bathtub

you lean back
you let the blood wash out of you

you open your hands
you let the weekend wash off of you

you drop your shoulders
you let the lyrics wash over you

seconds turn to minutes
minutes turn to hours
hours turn to regret

instincts

the psychologist asks
"what is your response to a threat?"
i try to fight but
my arms limp, my jaw slacks
"what is your response to?"
i try to fly but
my shoulders pop, my knees lock
"what is your response?"
i try to fawn but
my brow sticks, my eyes glaze
"what is yours?"
my skin is ice
"oh. freeze."

s.a.d. & g.a.d.

depression is intangible & abstract

depression is waiting
waiting for God knows what & God knows whom
stuck wading through neverending
options day after day
depression is interruptions
internalizing the toxic lines they feed me
winter after winter

anxiety is tangible & concrete

anxiety is weighing
weighing the thickening chain around my hips
the pinch & grip varying from hour to hour
at times lying
in a harmless pile at my feet
at times suffocating me just enough to crush me
without killing me
fall after fall

insomnia

at night, i am alone with my belly
watch it pout, bloated & heavy
thick with anxiety & lactose
tangled with menses & depression

i want to cry
beg & plead
with her to shrink

        to quiet

               to d i s a p p e a r

then i remember
how the future holds so much
she too is thick & tangled

come morning, she is gone
my wish, granted
her erasure, violent but temporary

disenchanted

i no longer dance
hang up my shoes
unlace all the strings
roll down my tights
undo all the buttons
slip off my dress
untie all the ribbons
release my tresses
& sink to the floor

anti-beatitudes

blessed are the bloody
for theirs is mythic pain

blessed are the chronic
for they will be gaslit

blessed are the disordered
for they will inherit the stigma

blessed are those who gnaw & gasp for relief
for they will be denied

blessed are the terminal
for they will obtain new terminology

blessed are the waitlisted
for the god committee will debate them

blessed are the pure in agony
for they will black out

blessed am i when doctors dehumanize me
repeatedly for the sake of their hypocritical oath
for mine, is this special hell

majik

curtains up, lights on, cameras flash
welcome one, welcome all
to my one woman show
show you all my tricks
reveal how i shapeshift
watch a black girl crawl out the womb
learn how to walk across hot coals
before she learns how to talk
still smiling, still breathing
watch a black girl grow wings
leap right into rings of fire
jump through hoops of applause
still smiling, still breathing
watch a black girl split in two
sing doublespeak to perfection
tap dance forty taps per second
still smiling, still breathing
now for the final act
the one you really came to see
watch the black girl vanish
before your emptied eyes
not one smile, not one single breath

new
moon

decay

i am fascinated by disintegration
the art of falling apart
ever since i could read & write
there was a magnetic draw

how do we descend into deterioration
so quick, so irreverent, so anticlimactic
the fade to black is no longer a fade
endings are so abrupt, so final, so

spirits

i came up short
you found me wanting

i became a ghost
you found me haunting

haunt you once, shame on me
haunt you twice, shame on we
haunt you next time, shame on who

cold hard want

i want you to burn kisses
into my shoulders
down my back
up my thighs
i want to see stars again

i want you over & over & over
against my better selves

this is senseless
i am running mad so
i retreat within myself
deeper & deeper still
i come close to the end but

halt

when i see

you. here
i thought i cast you out
i did not feel your presence
for days, weeks, months
but here you are
the last place i need you to be
the only place i want you to be

phrasing

i want you in every positive preposition
in me
by me
on me
plus me
with me
near me
along me
inside me
above me
across me
within me
beside me
astride me
around me
between me
throughout me

crushing

four months & one week & six days since our first date

i—

sob before falling into a drunken sleep
wake up at one thirty a.m. & cannot go back to sleep until five a.m.
cry silently in between
go back to sleep & have nightmare after nightmare
wake up at nine thirty a.m. & there is no call or message from you
spill more tears
will you to feel my hurt, so you call me at ten a.m.
you say you like me, but you do not want me

i—

hang up, feel nauseous
go to a meeting, feel sicker
take out the trash, almost trip
walk to the market, blubber over tomatoes
come back to my shower, sag under the wait
my face does not stop leaking, so i leave it running
for four days straight, one for each damn month

slipping

to the other fish in the sea:
it is not that your scales are not shiny
it is not that your curves are not smooth
it is not that your bodies are not warm
it is not that you stay in the shallows
it is not that you do not plunge into the deep

it is just that
i do not want other fish in the sea
i want the one that slipped away

the one that did not plunge into my deep
the one that stayed in my shallows
the one that warmed my curves & scales
the one that peeled all these layers & left me
smooth & shiny, gasping for air

unrequited

our, is nonexistent
us, is imaginary
we, simply cannot be

such a hopeless duet

you, never enough for me
me, always too much for you

i let go & i weep
forty days & forty nights
the heartache is all consuming

you & i ultimately capsize
sunk by words unsaid
& tears still unshed

(an)other woman

i am not her
i cannot be her
i will never ever be her

i am sculpted in obsidian
i run from ice & i am kissed by the fire
i grow dusky curls in a halo
i reflect a spectrum of sands in my eyes

she is not me
she cannot be me
she will never ever be me

she is molded in alabaster
she shuns fire & she is embraced by the ice
she grows handspun gold at her temple
she reflects a spectrum of skies in her eyes

her alabaster does not absorb
your inconsistencies
your excuses
your lies
the way my obsidian does

she stains too easily
she crumbles too quickly
she pales in comparison

but

you never saw the cracks on my surface
you never felt the dents in my curves
you never wanted to
did you

no sense

you will search for my eyes & nothing will be seen
you will call my name & no voice will be heard
you will reach for my hand & no warmth will be left
you will trace my scent & no wisp will be found
you will thirst for my love & not a drop will be tasted

you will lose all sense of me
nothing will look
nothing will sound
nothing will feel
nothing will smell
nothing will taste

the same

ever again

sometimes

i want to be violent

sometimes i want to throw a vase at the wall
scream as the petals float to the floor

sometimes i want to punch a mirror
count the cracks in my armor

sometimes i want to drag a chair
across the ground & smash it to pieces

sometimes i want to lose all control
destroy everything in my path

sometimes i want to prove them right
succumb to the rage & dissolve in the fury

sometimes i want to release all my pain
be the tsunami they fear me to be

what lurks within

are corners unseen that bury   the ugly
inside of you. most days   the ugly   is unprovoked
some days, like today,   the ugly   roars
the ugly   stalks out of the corners unveiled, rears its head
stares you down.   the ugly   absorbs your attention
the ugly   circles you in agonizing laps. scratches the floors
of your atria & leaves them raw.   the ugly   makes you grind
your teeth at the piercing sound.   the ugly   eats up space
in your mind &   the ugly   corrodes the beauty you fought
to preserve.   the ugly   decides your weak flesh is too familiar
& leaps outside. attacks your loves.   the ugly   forces you
to watch, horror-struck.   the ugly   leaves you to clean
up the collateral & pray no damage lasts from   the ugly

unhinged

the harsh clap of laughter
ringing in my memory
overcomes me & knocks me flat
runs off with my breath
takes & breaks me wide open

waxing
crescent

nile

[in the blue nile]

learn to wade in the sadness
this ancient river of moodiness
move with it, not against it
glide with it through rage or shine

[in the white nile]

let the water hold you & teach you
beauty of impermanence in each season
everything, always, is, changing
here one moment, elsewhere in another
nothing stops moving, not really
you will never be this same you again

juju

i cast a spell
inhale thoughts, exhale actions
feel the majik coursing through my body

cast a spell
to drain the cold out of my bones
wrap the shivers in my wool blanket

cast a spell
to iron the worry out of my skin
stamp the wrinkles in my yellow diary

cast a spell
to wring the sorrow out of my eyes
catch the drops in my alabaster box

cast a spell
to roll the lies out of my ears
toss the fluff in my old pillowcase

cast a spell
to flush the apologies out of my mouth
drown the emptiness in my jar of ink

willows

the willows are weeping
i curl up in their branches
sobbing into their leaves
they soothe me with their bony hands
like my grandmother of yesterday

the willows are weeping
i bury myself in their trunks
sewing myself in their stems
they shield me with their thick skin
like my mother of today

the willows are weeping
i intertwine myself in their roots
spreading out through their seeds
they follow me with their delicate feet
like my daughter of tomorrow

lineage

i see tamar
i see rahab
i see ruth
& i see their invisibility

i hear my great-grandmother
i hear my grandmother
i hear my mother
& i hear their silence

i speak for my daughter
i speak for my granddaughter
i speak for my great-granddaughter
& they rise through my voice

legacy

last week i had a dream in
runyankore
i cannot remember
what i said
or how i said it
i just know
what i said was
runyankore
for the first time in so long
i was speaking my mother's tongue
i could feel my grandmother laughing
i could feel my great-grandmother smiling
there were no melodies, no harmonies
in my words
i just dreamt in
runyankore
it was the first time since i was planted
in this amerikkka
it felt easy
it felt natural
i felt so close
to my grandmother
to my great-grandmother
for the first time since they left this earth

who invented the blues

look a here
look a here
sit on down
tell you a story if i can

big papa ragtime walked on by
big mama gospel let out a sigh

held on tight to
little girl blue
held on tight
& knew what to do

time went by
& little girl grew
time went by
& little girl flew

little lady saw
the great, wide world
little lady saw
the great, wide war

she stooped real low
back to old mama gospel
she cried real low
back with old mama gospel

took her some rest
put the sad on the strings
took all the rest
made honey from the sting

found her voice
knew just what to do
found her choice
now lady sings the blues

on blood & baptism

dear woman
they will teach you to fear blood
they will baptize you in shame
& condemn you as it flows
from within you
let the river flow
as it flows it shall cleanse
the scent is soft, the taste is sharp
the color is sour, the touch is sweet
they will never hear the river
they will not want to
you will not hear the river
you will not need to

dear woman
you will receive the Word
hide it in your heart & seek it as you walk
let it talk to you as you lie down
take up your cross
baptize yourself in the blood
take your tears & bathe yourself & be renewed
hold that deep breath within you
search yourself in the years when you do not exhale
remember your baptism
if you do not remember
your body will commemorate the occasion
perhaps thirteen times a year
you will not be alone

the tides will glide alongside you
the moon will guard you & count the days for you
you will push & your body will pull
you will pull & your body will push

on ink & injection

dear woman
you must rise
you must lift your eyes
you must pause
& then exhale
you see that blue
whether up or down, sky or sea
you will see that blue
the blues will not leave
for they are a part of you now
they are not you, they are just a part of you
you are not blue, the hue just colors all
you see

dear woman
string the incongruities together
let them pour from your soul
you must lose control—though you never had it
as the blood & the water pool within you
so they must flood out of you
let the streams rain down upon them
spare no one & no thing
let the remains of your baptism
be emptied from your being & begin again
make us comprehend your sorrow
sing us your story
show us that the siren is not out for blood
but seeks to baptize the sailor in her tears
that her very name is the sound of alarm

the sound of warning, to listen, to understand
that he must clear a path for your coming
you demand to take up space
you deserve to take up space

on periods & potions

dear woman
you must forgive yourself
you must retch & release all the self-abuse
that locked you in a war against yourself
you must kneel & exorcise the demons
that hold you ransom, that demand too high a price
you must open your eyes & let go of the water
that you absorbed since you left the womb
do not close your mouth, do not stand
do not close your eyes until every last drop
is free, until your self is fully emptied

dear woman
you must wash yourself
the pain will subside
but you must wash yourself in the blood
arise & reclaim what they stole from you
your voice, your choice
wade through the noise & take back
what is rightfully yours
the water will soothe
but only the blood will cleanse

dear woman
you will heal
do not forget that your body is borne of God
fashioned from the ancient
bound by stardust
do not forget the power of the scarlet rivers
rushing through your arteries & veins

dear woman
you can stand now
you are reborn & woven in light
how your skin missed being stroked by the sun
how your feet missed dancing with the water
how your tongue missed the kiss of salt
of how it heals thoroughly

conciliation

i give up
make friends with the anxiety
become close to the depression
take them to brunch & make it a monthly date
take them out to dinner during the harder weeks
we wine, we break bread, commiserate
we exchange different sides of the same story
laugh & cry at the disparity
they push me hard & i push
right back, left with accountability
they give me side eyes, i counter with eye rolls
we trade sharp inhales, gasp at the audacity of living
we pick apart my body & put it back together again
take them in stride, listen to their testimonies
with several grains of salt
take them in when no one else
can handle them
tuck them in the guest room
become gentle with anxiety
make peace with depression

my grief, observed

my grief looks different these days
some days it is hard & brittle like my nails
some days it is soft & malleable like my skin
some days it is coarse & twisted like my hair

some days, oh some days, i cannot find it
all i can do is feel it, but not quite touch it
all i can do is feel it, but not quite hold it

some days it is gaseous, fills up the whole room
without being visible
without being tasted
without being smelled

some days it shrieks at me
some days i savage in return

& it takes it & takes it & takes & takes
takes every bite, every shot, every punch
sometimes it punches back

some days we just hold each other
some days we sleep on opposite ends of the bed
some days we sleep in opposite rooms of the house

some days, oh these are the good days
we go out for the fun of it
we go for hours

grief takes off my coat
grief holds my hand

we talk
share thoughts, share fears
share laughter, share tears

how i long for these days

timely

i think of timing
the before & the after
the ante meridiem & post meridiem
the firsts & the lasts, the surprise of it all
the gone too soons & left too lates
i think of straight lines
the fact that time as we know it is cyclical
the fact that time as we know it is enigmatic

i think of timing
the earlys & the delays
the beginnings & the endings
the forevers & the nevers, the binary of it all
the things of the past & the things of the future
i think of circles
what if time does not move in a straight line
what if time does not end with death
what if time does not end at all

what if death is not the opposite of life
but simply a shift in time

begotten

does the sadness beget sin
or does the sin make me sad

which comes first, the sinner or the sadness

does the madness beget mercy
or does the mercy make me mad

which comes next, the mercy or the madness

does the gladness beget grace
or does the grace make me glad

which comes last, the grace or the gladness

sabbath

where are pockets of rest in the swell of exhaustion
where are remnants of peace in the chaos of revolution
you say i must make time for rest & space for peace
i am trying, i am trying, i am trying
i am failing, i am failing, i am failing
God can hear my cries, but i fell silent long ago
God can see my tears, but i ran dry long ago
where is abundance in the face of scarcity
where is celebration in the arms of lament
& yet
i recall the eucharist
i remember the bread & the wine
i am breaking, i am breaking, i am breaking
i am healing, i am healing, i am healing

icon

i wonder
how he looked
how he sounded
how he felt
how he smelled
how he tasted

i wonder
if my Christ on the cross
was the Christ you paint him to be

half
moon

too much

my greatest fear
is not that i am not enough
rather
my greatest fear
really
my greatest accusation
is that i am too much

too soft
too loud
too open

for my own good

what you really mean is
for your own good

you make goodness a zero-sum game
you discard subjectivity & relativity
your framework, your mathematics
your very mind is
so limited
so threatened
by my goodness
that you reduce me
to your one-dimensional perspective

you too could partake in the muchness
you too could share in the goodness
but you reject it & try
to shrink it to your limits

gwe ndeka, iwe ondekye
i am not too much for me
you are not enough for you

spit her out

open your mouth & give back the girl
you swallowed long before she was a woman

scrape your tongue & give back the words
you stole that left her speechless

cough until it burns & give back the voice
you ripped from her throat

open your mouth & let the woman
reclaim the birthright of the girl

spit. her. out.

switch

you smile as your body loosens
you use your bare hands
your godless bare hands
& you take part of me
& you wait for me to die
i do not

i smile as my body tightens
i use my bare hands
my godful bare hands
& i take back all of me
& i wait for you die
you do

~~virgin~~

this is how
      they branded
bodies of women:
      they discarded
used lipstick
      they trashed
smeared cake
      they cracked
shared lollipops
      they melted
bitten chocolate
      they dumped
cups of saliva
      they tore
dirty napkins
      they ripped
old dishrags
      they burned
stained sheets
      they bartered
unwrapped gifts
      they crushed
plucked roses
      they uprooted
crumpled daisies
      they buried
opened caves

they claim
no one will want you after that
they warn
no one will love you after that
they threaten
God will hate you after that

you are not food
you are not clothing
you are not shelter
for the bodies of men

you are human
you are a sacred thing
you are body, mind, spirit

their ancestors will never rewrite your name
our descendants will never forget your name

shedding

they tell me it takes twenty-seven days
to shed my skin & start anew

so be it

i have calculated the minutes
i have counted the hours
i have marked the date

wednesday
just after two a.m.
on the third of april
i will host a party for you
open a bottle of pinot noir
set two glasses & plates at the table
& take your skeleton out of my closet

you will offer your hollow apologies
i will let them fall & scatter at my feet

i will toast to your failure to unravel me
as you crumble to dust & fade to ashes
not a trace of your memory
left upon me

blooming

the third of april came & went
no wine, no party, no apology
for the first time in my life
i chose to celebrate life in peak bloom
the cherry blossoms were dressed
in full regalia, so i took a train
to the river & danced
with the floating petals
mastered the art of letting go
so i could bear fruits of change
wandered to a rock & dangled
my feet over green waters, drank
in the brightening sun, ushered in
the warmer seasons, welcomed
my brand new skin

notes to self

music for lovers is lovely
but music reminiscent of your unrequited love
must be placed on a shelf in a hidden room. for now
maybe one day you can make the song all your own
in the meantime, find other harmonies
to soothe your soul

sing to yourself
on your loneliest nights, sing to the moon
she is always present, though you may not always see her
she will weave your melodies into the fabric of the tide
she will listen while your heart learns to love again

play the strings
let each chord speak for you
place your fears & securities
your doubts & certainties
your dreams & realities
place them on all three of the clefs, alto included
lay them to rest for as many measures as needed

rocketeer

i take some time to explore the universe of my mind
practice giving myself space to roam between
different galaxies. discover new planets housing
childhood fantasies, secret maladies, forgotten symphonies
fall for the constellations of my prayers

weather my tether as i map the patterns
mark the gaps. follow my thoughts all the way
to the end, especially if they scare me. realize no one
will hear me scream where sound does not travel
finally seek help when the black holes overwhelm me

i forgive myself for failing to love the dark matter
grow to respect the unknown & let it be
become grateful for the redeeming speed of light
feel humbled that the human mind can be
infinite, dark, spectacular—a whole universe unto itself

questioning

who, i wonder at the stars
you will know once they leave
what, i sigh at the clouds
you will see what you want to see
when, i whine to the moon
you will only heal after you consent
where, i plead with the rain
you will find it deep within you
why, i croon to the ocean
you will need to let go
how, i whisper to the wind
you will learn by listening

spacing

i am at home in the sky
live in limbo & spend time in transit
sleep babylike at high elevation
float easy through the stratosphere

body at rest, weightless
airplanes are a second home
lost my first one, settled on this one
clock stops at cruising altitude

do my best writing in the clouds
borne from dreamscapes
so my words are lighter than air
though they weave cirrus
they hold the weight of stratus

make my best words while equatorial
born of savanna & rainforest
so my words are hotter than fire
while they burn streaks like lava
they can exfoliate like pumice

the first snow

is delicate
for the first time since birth
i feel delicate
for the first time altogether
i say the words out loud
but first
i turn the words over
in my mouth
really taste how light they are
i decide i like the taste

may i never lose the wonder
of this bright, cold earth
may i hold it nearer & dearer
as it melts away
may i see every crystal
in sharp clarity
may i feel every pinch
in full lucidity

baltimore

i was not allowed to fall in love with her

i was told she was not romantic
but she gave me the best kiss of my life

i was told she was rough around the edges
but she held my softness with gentleness

i was told she only saw the ugliness within
but she called me the prettiest girl in the world

i was told she only knew tragedy
but she taught me how to heal

yet i was not allowed to fall in love with her

waxing
gibbous

first kisses

we lived next to each other on the street
spun skirts next to each other in the heat

we laughed together after the caning at school
swam together in bikinis in the shallow pool

we loved grape soda on the longer weekends
spilled grape soda on the pretty pink bunk beds

mortar & pestle

      at six, i am still too small
for maama's acrylic apron
      reach up on my tippiest toes
dip my finger in the mchuzi mix
      we begin thin once she glides in
rolls the mandazi & the kabalagala
      grinds out the karo & posho
conjures her signature stew
      teaches me to holy my first supper
peppered omelet turned rolex
      whispers all her secret ingredients
sprinkles in her majik tricks
      ushers my hands to lay down the yolk
speaks only in hums as she is kneading

anansi

i spin a thousand & one secrets
into the seams of my words
i spin many a wish & many a dream
in between the lines
i spin a grand mosaic with stories
that remain hidden to the naked eye
i spin a whirlwind of emotions
into the very punctuation & there
there they can find release

tongues

i am a woman of many tongues
delicate with my words
use a pair of tongs to take them
out of my mouth
lay them gently in the world

i was born with two tongues
learned the third one before i could walk
flexed all three as i learned to talk

my strongest tongue is foreign
walks & talks like the colonizer
added two more tongues to my armory
two more colonizers: the unholy trinity
of guns & germs & steel

saltwater has eroded the two tongues
gifted to me at birth. oceans
washed the accents away
diluted the cadence

now i lie alone at night
stretch as far as i can
into my memory
stunned by what i see
i recognize my mother tongues
but they do not recognize me

i want to pour my last words
from the same cup as my first words
let that be my final hallelujah
my holy elegy

at least, i still know how to cry in runyankore
at least, i still know how to laugh in luganda

t.c.k.

you made a trade
mudpies for snowballs
pigweed for ragweed
flame lilies for water lilies
acacia trees for hickory trees
sunshowers for hailstorms
landslides for earthquakes
wet season for equinox
dry season for solstice
nile for mississippi

you lost so much, beloved
you gained so much, beloved

silver linings

ode to my second suburb
where i had box braids in the winter
where i had senegalese twists in the summer
where the highways are always under construction
where orange slices & apple juice are aplenty
where blue minivans & beige sedans are the norm
where sparkling cider & sweet potatoes abound
where string orchestra concerts still my mind
where gua bao & boba make me content
where the cul-de-sac throws block parties
where miso & gyoza are my small joys
where annual book fairs make me giddy
where yuzu & bulgogi are my happy place
where trees are lush & everlasting
where pho & banh bao make my heart smile
where ponds & streams are abundant
where samosas & paratha make my spirit dance

have you told you

have you told you lately that you love you
no really, have you
last thursday during the double shift
three years ago on your birthday, never

have you told you lately that you love you
no really, have you
last friday when you were drunk
two years ago at her wedding, never

have you told you lately that you love you
no really, have you
last saturday when you were high
one year ago at his funeral, never

have you told you lately that you love you
no really, have you
last sunday during the sermon
this year at a new year's party, today

alternate versions

       he grazes me in major key
she brushes me in sharp
       he touches me in lofi
she strokes me in flat
       he holds me in stripped
she caresses me in hifi
       he embraces me in reverb
she wraps me in minor key

both &

amethyst is just as purple
as lavender is just as purple
as lilac is just as purple
as magenta is just as purple
as mauve is just as purple
as plum is just as purple
as
v
i
o
l
e
t

buried treasure

why steal my heart
when you can
embark on a greater quest
why steal my heart
when you can
read the signs of my body
wander the paths of my mind
follow the rhapsodies of my soul
& land at the door in awe
as i offer you room
in this heart of pure gold
with arms wide open

intertwined

i will love you so honestly
my love will be so sincere
that you will be stripped bare
reduced to nothing but truth

i will tell you truth so wholly
my truth will be so complete
that you will be utterly breathless
reduced to nothing but love

swan songs

on this tenth anniversary
of your grandmothers' deaths
pack a suitcase, buy a one-way ticket
to the motherland
the first hills you called home
leave the airport, pass the city, drive into the dusk
open the door to the bungalow, breathe in the dust
sit on the narrow bed, tenderly, lay out the dresses

nestle the green & blue silk
wonder what her favorite color was
slip on the gomesi, walk to jajja's grave first
webale nyo, jajja, thank you so much
you tell her all about your life across the ocean
she listens in with a furrow & a smile, she always listened
you beg her to remind you what her voice sounds like, she laughs
at least you still remember what her posho tastes like
but you never attempt to recreate it
you tell her that her son still smiles, loves you quiet
you tell her that her son is nothing like her husband
she listens with a furrow & a sigh
your throat burns with questions
overflows with things to say
so let the tears speak for you
welaba, jajja, goodbye until next time

return to the bungalow

nestle the orange & red satin
wonder what her favorite color was
slip on the kitenge, walk to kaaka's grave last
webare munonga, kaaka, thank you so much
you tell her all about your life across the ocean
she chimes in with a dimple & a smile, she always chimed
you beg her to remind you what her voice sounds like, she laughs
at least you still remember what her karo tastes like
but you never attempt to recreate it
you tell her that her daughter still smiles, loves you fierce
you tell her that her daughter is nothing like her husband
she listens with a dimple & a sigh
your stomach aches for answers
runs out of things to say
so let the tears speak for you
sibegye, kaaka, goodbye until next time

full
moon

epiphany

i feel it now, i understand
i am the key to my healing
i must inhale & search for me
i am the antidote

as i release my pasts, i release my own poison
as I receive my futures, i receive my own forgiveness

i feel it now, i understand
i am the answer to my prayer
i must exhale & make room for me
i am the miracle

apology letter to my body

i apologize

for the scratching at the stretch marks
for burning off the scars
for scorching the curls

for letting them convince me to go to war
against my own body
for refusing to forfeit
for shrinking myself more & more

for clawing at you
for screaming at you
for abusing you

i do not truly love you, not yet
i was told others cannot know
how to fully love you until i do
i hope learning how to love you
can teach me how to love others too

so

i promise to exhale
i promise to be patient on long days
i promise to be gentle on rough days
i promise not to rush you, to hush you
i promise to finally be your friend

forgive me for not loving you as i ought to
for if God made the beautiful stars & this body too
beauty can be found in this body, through & through

thank you letter to my body

thank you for waiting
waiting so long to just let go
you struggle as your hands loosen
you wince as you fall
you tell yourself the ending will be worth the wait
you finally believe it

thank you for wrestling
wrestling is hard
fear & trembling become strangely familiar
you are left to wonder when it ends
if it ends, how it ends
you carry so much, you must lay it down
you tarry so much, you must not become the weight
you will not become it

thank you for being
being is a gift you must learn to receive
you open yourself
you see yourself, actually see yourself
for the first time
& it is Good

thank you for trying to see yourself
the way God sees you
the scales will fall off your eyes
thank you for trying to hold yourself
the way God holds you
the calluses will fade in time
you'll see

love letter to my body

she is not broken
fragile, but not broken
her curls are not cinnamon for consuming
but umber twists at her temple
they guard a labyrinth of a mind, inside
her eyes are not honey for consuming
but rich mahogany, reaching high
they are framed by saturn's rings themselves
no telescope needed
her lips are not toffee for consuming
but ancient terracotta of her seven hills
they dance like the gentle grooves
of the sahara's dunes
her skin is not cacao for consuming
but contours of bronze
they shine in the sun
built from an age all of their own
she is timeless
fragile, but timeless

thank God for the dark

oh to see my dark eyes
twirl my dark curls
feel my dark skin
sync the dark blood coursing within
gratitude for my shadow which
after all, has always been
oh to touch the dark matter that threads the sky
cloaks me in warmth & wild to
tread the dark ocean beyond
what eye can see, hand can feel
oh to kiss the charcoal that cleanses
the soot that sanctifies above
gratitude for my scarred feet beneath
the dark earth that holds us all to gather

long live the *queen*

we are sage & savanna
we salt this broken earth
we all kinds of womanist
we are return to sender
leave white jesus to the west
we are language & limber
we are *asantewaa* (1840)

we are ruthless & raw
we are vengeance
with or without the lord
we turn conquest to consequence
wipe that jungle fever off your face
we are black girl juju
we are *ranavalona* (1778)

we are matriarchy
we are blood & beads
we are soaked in secrets
we talk turmeric & tea
we are babies on our back
we are built for the crown
we are *nandi* (1760)

we are alto & agony
we are music, from twists
to toes, we be music
we are clay & candlelight
we are daughters of dichotomy
we are warrior from the womb
we are *nzinga* (1663)

we are hallelujah & honey
we are water turned into wine
we smooth skin & sucker punch
we are light you on fire
for burning our birthright
we are divinity
we are *aminatu* (1610)

we are spitfire & sand dunes
we are dancing in the dark
we are cassava & cloves
we are raw & unrelenting
we are full-bodied alchemist
we are dismantle
we are *gudit* (960)

we are curls on curls
we made of stretch & mark
we are baobab & basket
we are layers upon layers
we are the cup & the overflow
we are grace incarnate
we are *amanitore* (50)

we were seeds

zora

       maya

           toni

did not bleed on the page

did not sweat between the words

did not cry through the letters

for this guilt

       for this shame

           for this fear

in no particular order

hold your body, cradle your self in your own arms. as you hug every fragment, study each one. hold them to the light. then bind them together with gold. may the scars glitter & fill you with wonder like the stars above.

examine the landscape of your body. become familiar with the scenery. stand before a large mirror. strip. as you peel off each layer, gently run your hands over your skin, your hair, your nails. as the last thread floats off your body, look up at the mirror & drink in the vision before you. do a little dance & marvel at how the landscape shifts.

cleanse the rubble of the past from your body. do so patiently. the pieces are laced between your gargantuan heart, remember? as the toxins, the dead skin, the excess pool at your feet, give thanks for seasons & develop an appreciation for cycles. bathe in the beauty of forgiveness & wash yourself in grace. rinse & repeat as needed.

drink up. you have emptied yourself to start over, so replenish your body. you are made of mostly water, so fill yourself with mostly water. conjure lavish blends. learn to make your drinks from scratch. harvest your own ingredients if you can. embrace a lifestyle of fresh-squeezed & home-brewed. toast to yourself as you master moderation.

savor your daily bread. fill your body with the fresh & colorful. sample the cuisines of all cultures. relish every bite & sensation. feast on the flavors offered by our tender earth. plant some by the window & blend your own in the kitchen. teach your body to crave homemade goodness. cultivate an intimate relationship with food.

rise. seek out your body's happy place. it may be the woods or the water, the studio or the slopes. find your space & become familiar with it. gather up your energy & open your body. move with intentionality. exchange tight for loose & finetune your technique. push for daily effort. experience the miracle of the physical. your body is a force of nature, harness that power.

rest. the creator created a day just for rest but creation needs it every day. your body will not last forever. treat it as such. listen to the warning bells & look out for the red flags. study your circadian rhythms & protect your sleep cycle. understand that you also need to rest while you are awake. note that being idle is not the same as being rested.

alchemize. eden may be hidden but the majik remains. find her remnants in the raw, unrefined, organic, whole. extract carefully. wrap your skin in heavenly scents. nourish your hair with pure oils. strengthen your nails with rich vitamins.

unroll your hippocampus. decode & deconstruct the memories as they unfold. embrace the crest of feeling, the trough of emotion. preserve the fingerprints left on your heart. breathe, beloved. accept that healing is not linear. for now, you are still here.

my kinda girl

she is my kinda girl

sings her best in the shower kinda girl
loops the chorus in the mirror kinda girl
cries her heart out in the bathtub & then
hums her favorite hymn kinda girl
always finds the harmony
caged bird kinda girl

she is my kinda girl

acting feels like breathing kinda girl
knows the lines by heart kinda girl
whispers the monologue in her sleep & then
breaks your heart on stage kinda girl
lives for make-believe
storyteller kinda girl

she is my kinda girl

dances to any beat kinda girl
feet need to feel the world kinda girl
runs barefoot in thunderstorms & then
builds up to a hurricane kinda girl
gonna fly away any day now
broken shackles kinda girl

the sea & me

i want to make love to the sea

i want to take her in my arms
laugh as she slips through them

i want to wrap myself in her scent
shiver when she kisses my feet

i want to sleep with her at midnight
ask her if she still longs for the moon

i want to swim in her depths
sink to the bottom of her bed

& never come up for air

for late bloomers

here is to you, my late bloomer
you were tended with such care
& as your body grew
it was in no hurry to do so
as others blossomed around you
your leaves quietly exhaled
your roots stretched slowly
& your buds stayed stubborn
in your garden of friends
you danced closer to the ground
glad you took your time, dear one
you stunned them without making a sound

she

is the anomaly
the one in billions
she aimed for the sun

but did not land

among the stars
she was swallowed
whole, by the moon

Acknowledgments

Grateful to our one & only moon.

Grateful to the ocean, the seven cities, the fifteen streets that shaped me.

Grateful to God, to my partner, to my siblings, to my best friends, to my close friends. You are, for me, a reflection of the Divine.

Grateful to my foremothers, Alison & Amelia, Joy & Joyce, Edna & Suza. Grateful to every ancestor whose blood, sweat, tears softened the path for me.

Grateful to my language & literature teachers, especially Teacher Florence & Teacher Heidi. You made me feel seen.

Grateful to my undergraduate professors, especially Cliff & Andrew. Your loving-kindness lifts me up.

Grateful to my graduate professors, especially Tracie & Elizabeth. You made me feel heard.

Grateful to my agent & my editor. Your commitment to my work changed my life.

Grateful to the editors of the *Kodon*, *Kiwi Collective Magazine*, *Protest Through Poetry*, *Solstice Literary Magazine*, *Black Poetry Review*, *Yellow Arrow Journal*, who first published earlier versions of several poems tucked in this book.

Grateful to all the unknown & unnamed beings who loved me out of the lows, who loved me into the highs, who loved this book into existence.

Grateful to you, of course, dear reader or dear listener. Your time & space are a precious gift to me.

About the Author

Tramaine Suubi is a multilingual writer from Kampala. Tramaine is a graduate of the Iowa Writers' Workshop.